IELTS SPEAKING PART 2 STRATEGIES

The Ultimate Guide With Tips, Tricks, And Practice On How To Get A Target Band Score Of 8.0+ In 10 Minutes A Day

RACHEL MITCHELL

Copyright © 2017

All rights reserved.

ISBN: 9781549720192

TEXT COPYRIGHT © [RACHEL MITCHELL]

all rights reserved. No part of this guide may be reproduced in any form without permission in writing from the publisher except in the case of brief quotations embodied in critical articles or reviews.

Legal & disclaimer

The information contained in this book and its contents is not designed to replace or take the place of any form of medical or professional advice; and is not meant to replace the need for independent medical, financial, legal or other professional advice or services, as may be required. The content and information in this book have been provided for educational and entertainment purposes only.

The content and information contained in this book have been compiled from sources deemed reliable, and it is accurate to the best of the author's knowledge, information, and belief. However, the author cannot guarantee its accuracy and validity and cannot be held liable for any errors and/or omissions. Further, changes are periodically made to this book as and when needed. Where appropriate and/or necessary, you must consult a professional (including but not limited to your doctor, attorney, financial advisor or such other professional advisor) before using any of the suggested remedies, techniques, or information in this book.

Upon using the contents and information contained in this book, you agree to hold harmless the author from and against any damages, costs, and expenses, including any legal fees potentially resulting from the application of any of the information provided by this book. This disclaimer applies to any loss, damages or injury caused by the use and application, whether directly or indirectly, of any advice or information presented, whether for breach of contract, tort, negligence, personal injury, criminal intent, or under any other cause of action.

You agree to accept all risks of using the information presented inside this book.

You agree that by continuing to read this book, where appropriate and/or necessary, you shall consult a professional (including but not limited to your doctor, attorney, or financial advisor or such other advisor as needed) before using any of the suggested remedies, techniques, or information in this book.

TABLE OF CONTENT

Introduction
Part 2 Speaking Introduction
Part 2 Speaking Tips
People Description
Adjectives of Personality
People Description Model Answer
Model Sentences for People Description
Place Description
Adjectives for Describing Places
Place Description Model Answer
Model Sentences for Place Description
Object Description
Useful Adjectives For Describing Objects
Object Description Model Answer
Model Sentences For Object Description
Past Event Description
Past Event Description Model Answer
Model Sentences for Past Event Description
Conclusion
Check Out Other Books

INTRODUCTION

Thank you and congratulate you for downloading the book *"IELTS Speaking Part 2 Strategies: The Ultimate Guide with Tips, Tricks and Practice on How to Get a Target Band Score of 8.0+ in 10 Minutes a Day."*

This book is well designed and written by an experienced native teacher from the USA who has been teaching IELTS for over 10 years. She really is the expert in training IELTS for students at each level. In this book, she will provide you all proven Formulas, Tips, Tricks, Strategies, Explanations, Structures, Part 2 Speaking Language, Vocabulary and Model Part 2 Answers to help you easily achieve an 8.0+ in the IELTS Part 2 Speaking, even if your speaking is not excellent. This book will also walk you through step-by-step on how to develop your well-organized answers for the Part 2 Speaking; clearly analyze and explains the different types of cue card topics that are asked for Part 2 Speaking; provide you step-by-step instructions on how to answer each type of cue card topic excellently.

As the author of this book, Rachel Mitchell believes that this book will be an indispensable reference and trusted guide for you who may want to maximize your band score in IELTS Part 2 Speaking. Once you read this book, I guarantee you that you will have learned an extraordinarily wide range of useful, and practical IELTS Part 2 Speaking strategies and formulas that will help you become a successful IELTS taker as well as you will even become a successful English user in work and in life within a short period of time only.

Take action today and start getting better scores tomorrow!

Thank you again for purchasing this book, and I hope you enjoy it.

PART 2 SPEAKING INTRODUCTION

When part 1 speaking is finished; this means after the examiner has asked you a series of questions on three different topics *(work, study, where are you living, and the two other topics)*, they are going to move to part 2 speaking, they will give you a direction, they will explain exactly what they are doing, everything is very clear in part 2 speaking. The examiner will be giving you a card, and the card will have a task on it. They want you to talk about something.

What do they want you to talk about?

That will be **NOUNS**: people, places, things like objects that you own, objects that you would like to own, events (things that you did in the past, for example, *graduation ceremony, grandpa's birthday, etc.*)

The examiner will give you a card and ask you to describe something, someone, a place, or an event, and your job is to take this card and you are going to talk about the card for 2 minutes. Another word is that you are going to give a short speech. They are **not** asking you questions in part 2 speaking. It's different from part 1 speaking (questions and answers). In part 2 speaking, just has answer, no question.

When the examiner gives you a card, they also give you a piece of paper and a pencil or a pen to take notes. You will have 1 minute to look at the card and think about what you are going to say and you can take notes in that 1 minute. Remember that you can use the notes to read and look at while you are speaking. You must talk about the topic on the card, but you can freely talk about anything. They will make this card general enough that everyone can talk about. So they are **not** going to say *"talk about your favorite city in Egypt"*, so it's never so specific. Instead, they just ask you to *"talk about your favorite city"*. Everyone can think about their favorite city. It's very general. It's a good idea to talk about the topic points in order. Here is the thing, before you are talking about something is challenging on the card because part 2 will offer some unique challenging points, I want you to start thinking about simple points on the card first. These are basic questions because you can add a question mark to these, change the words around and these are all questions. These are actually part 1 speaking questions.

Example:

Do you have a favorite book?

Yes, I really love Harry Porter

Who wrote it?

This book was written by J. K. Rowling. She is a British author who is now very famous for writing this book.

What happens in the book?

Well, a lot of things are happening in the book. Basically, it's about a boy, Harry, who discovers he has a magical power…

When did you read it?

I first read this book since I was 14 years old…

What I am doing here is I am trying to produce extended answers to part 1 speaking questions. That's a key here. **Do not** think of this as a 2-minute speech; that's too much. Instead, think of it as 10 seconds, 10 seconds, 20 seconds, 20 seconds, 20 seconds, and 20 seconds. Little pieces are more important.

There are some challenges in part 2 speaking. One of the big challenges coming up with an idea is that you don't know what they are going to give you on a card. It could be anything. Some things are easy to prepare for, other things are weird.

For example: *Are you ready to talk about your favorite comic actor?* **May be not**.

Who is the comic actor? You might **not be ready** to talk about this topic, and in order to choose a good thing to talk about is also a challenge.

The other thing is taking notes and using them. The only purpose of these notes is for you. You don't receive a band score for taking notes. The examiner will not collect it, and they will throw it into the trash. So the only purpose that the notes have is for you to be using while you are speaking.

You <u>don't have to write sentences on your piece of paper</u> because you have very limited time. Instead, you should <u>write keywords</u>, and <u>1, 2 or 3 phrases</u> that when you look at the words, they give you ideas for other things to talk about.

So if you are going to answer *"why is it your favorite book?"*

You could say: ***it's exciting***, and then explain <u>why it is exciting</u> by looking at your notes and start talking. Looking at keywords will allow you to talk a lot of things about your favorite book.

Sample answer:

Today I'm gonna tell you about Harry porter, one of my favorite books. <u>This novel is written by J. K. Rowling</u>. She is now a famous British author. <u>In fact</u>, this was the first book that she ever wrote. In this book, I meet my hero Harry Porter, he is a young boy <u>who</u> finds out that he has a magical power, <u>therefore</u> he goes to school to develop his power and learn skills that using poison…..<u>I first read this book 15 years ago</u> during the winter time <u>when</u> the weather was really cold outside. I got this book for Christmas, <u>my friend had recommended it to me</u> because he had read it and really enjoyed it…<u>I love this book because it's so exciting</u>. What I mean is there are a lot of amazing adventures and powers…it's really well written, and has a lot of interesting things to read. And finally, I really like Harry, he is a really friendly and charming boy…..<u>actually</u>, I really like to read this book.

Answer structure: *Explaining -- adding ideas -- explaining -- examples*

Another challenge in part 2 speaking is a lack of question. In part 2 speaking, there is no question, so what you need to do is to show the examiner *where you are talking about? How you are talking? Signal and pause* can allow you <u>to be a lot more organized</u>, take a breath and allow the examiner to easily find you while you are speaking.

How the examiner marks you in part 2 speaking:

- **Coherence and cohesion:** are you *speaking smoothly* (not ~~too quickly~~) and *in an organized way* that is *easy to understand*.
- **Vocabulary:** are you using *a wide range of words, verb forms?* Are you *being descriptive?* Are you *paraphrasing?* Is your *vocabulary accurate?*

- **Grammar:** sentence structures; *concession & contrast*; *conditionals* (it depends…); *verb tenses* (using a range of verb tenses); *verb forms*; *adjectives* (be descriptive + explain adjectives); *referencing & pronouns*.
- **Pronunciation** (focus on the *final sounds, intonation, word stress*)

PART 2 SPEAKING TIPS

Remember to include a clear introduction and conclusion to your Part 2 speech.

Introduction:

- *I'm going to describe...*
- *The X I would like to describe...*
- *I'm going to talk about an X (in my country called the...)*

Conclusion:

- *That's why the ... is such a famous building.*
- *It's a very famous X not only within my country but also abroad.*
- *It's such a special X because...*

Continuation:

If you find yourself having nothing to say in the middle of your talk, take a moment to refocus by using one of the useful phrases like:

- *Let me think...*
- *Well,...*
- *Actually,...*
- *I can't quite remember the ...*
- *I think ...*
- *I mean...*
- *Basically,...*
- *Anyway, ...*

Do you need eye contact in IELTS speaking?

There is nothing in the IELTS exam that has anything about eye contact. Of course, you want to keep some eye contact with the examiner. This is polite but you've got some notes in front of you that you took, you've got the card in front of you. You're speaking, you're reading the notes, and you're thinking about more things to say. You've got a lot of things going on. In the exam, this is quite more important. Looking at the examiner and keeping some eye contact with him **is NOT important**. I would say if you worry about it, you should *stay focused, stay focused, stay focused* and *look at the examiner every once in a while*. When the examiner gives you a minute to take notes, take your notes. The examiner will tell you when your time is up. Please don't take notes and say *"can I have more time?"* – It **never happens**. Likewise, when your 1 minute is up, the examiner will say *"your time is up"*, and now you can start your speaking.

The keyword of part 2 speaking is *being organized, being organized* and *being organized* so the examiner can follow what you are talking about and *try to be influent, try to produce a lot of English for 2 minutes*. Be strict with your time when you practice, don't ever give your short speech for over 2 minutes.

Most common things we usually do in part 2 speaking is **a place, a person, an event, an experience, or an object.**

If you are describing **a place**, you should provide some details like *where is it located? When did you first go there? What does it look like? What happened there? Why you were there? What you did there? How did you feel about this place? Why did you remember this place so well? What do you remember the most about this place? Why do you think this place is so beautiful?*

Pay attention to the verb tenses (present tense, past tense…)

PEOPLE DESCRIPTION

When you describe a person, you should try to use <u>adjectives of evaluation</u> and <u>adjectives of personality</u>.

- *Who the person is?* (Relatives or friend...)
  I would like to talk about <u>my grandmother</u>.
  I would like to talk about <u>my favorite history teacher</u>.
  I would like to talk about <u>my next door neighbor</u>.
- *What do they do?* (occupation)
- *Social position* (what do they do in society?)
- *How do you know them?*
- *What they are like* (using <u>adjectives of personality</u> & <u>explain the adjectives</u>).
  If you tell the examiner someone is <u>strict and hardworking, give them examples about how they are strict and hardworking</u> *"I admire my father, but sometimes he is quite strict. What I mean is if I am 5 minutes late for dinner, he makes me give him a dollar"*. So what you should do is you need to have an explanation because if you don't, it makes the listener naturally feel like that <u>they are missing something</u>. Imagine that you have a conversation with your friend. He is very polite, and he asks you *"how was your holiday?"* and you say *"well, I had a lot of fun. I went to London. It's very interesting"*. Then, certainly, your friend will be asking to himself *"interesting? How?" what do you mean for "interesting"?* So, you must explain your adjectives. You <u>don't need to use a lot of adjectives</u>, you <u>just need maybe 2, maybe 3 adjectives but you must explain them</u>.
  If you just throw out the adjectives *"Oh, I love my father because he is so humorous, friendly, hardworking, thrifty..."* that means you are just <u>listing</u> and certainly that's <u>not impressive</u>; that <u>doesn't sound natural</u>.
- *What they have achieved* (using <u>phrases of achievement</u>). These are used a lot in part 2 speaking because in part 2 speaking, we usually talk about people that we like or we admire and we have relationship with)

PHRASES THAT TALK ABOUT **WORKING HARD**:

Through sheer hard work, he has built up his company

My mother was not very successful in high school, but she *persevered* and graduated from university. Now she is a doctor.

PHRASES THAT TALK ABOUT **SUCCESS**:

He *has the will to succeed*.

Something I admire about Barack Obama is he *earned a respect of people* who met him.

PHRASES THAT TALK ABOUT **TALENT**:

He *has a gift for* playing guitar.

He *has a gift for* kicking football.

My mother *has a gift for* cooking.

PHRASES THAT TALK ABOUT **ADMIRATION**:

I really *appreciate* what my father did for me.

I will always *look up to/ admire/ respect* him for his work.

I *think highly of/ proud of* my father and his work.

EXPRESSIONS HOPING TO IMITATE SOMEBODY:

I hope I am as + adjective + as + person

I hope I will be as + adjective + as + person

I hope I am *as successful as* my father is when I grow up

I hope I am *as beautiful as* my mother is when I grow up.

I hope I will be *as wealthy as* Bill Gates.

EXPRESSIONS OF IMITATION:

I would like to be as intelligent as my grandfather.

I would like to be as beautiful as my grandfather.

I would like to be as wealthy as Bill Gates.

ADJECTIVES OF PERSONALITY

NEGATIVE PERSONALITY ADJECTIVES LIST

Aggressive: *He has a real passive aggressive personality/ he had a very aggressive attitude.*

Arrogant: *He was so arrogant that he thought he could tell everyone what to do.*

That girl is arrogant because of her beauty.

Bitchy: *She can be really bitchy sometimes.*

Boastful: *Peter was too boastful when describing his new bike.*

Boring: *I don't like Tom because he is boring and unfriendly.*

Bossy: *I dislike her because she is bossy.*

Careless: *Although he is brave, he is careless.*

Changeable: *She is changeable and stubborn.*

Conservative: *He is not as conservative as he used to be.*

Cowardly: *Tom is shy and cowardly.*

Nervous: *He was nervous so he forgot her name.*

Obsessive: *He was obsessive about food and coffee.*

Overemotional: *She was overemotional in public.*

Pessimistic: *He is pessimistic about the future*

Quick-tempered: *My brother is quick-tempered and impatient.*

Resentful: *She is resentful about being demoted.*

Others: Rude, selfish, silly, stingy, sneaky, stubborn, timid, unkind, unreliable, unkind, immature, short-temper = irritable, frugal = thrifty, cruel, deceitful, dishonest, evil, flirtatious, foolish, fussy, greedy, grumpy, impatient, impolite, inconsiderate, intolerant, inflexible, indecisive, lazy, jealous, materialistic, mean, moody, narrow-minded, naughty, nasty, etc.

POSITIVE PERSONALITY ADJECTIVES LIST

Affectionate: *She is affectionate to her animals.*

Ambitious: *He is ambitious to succeed.*

Friendly: *Tom is friendly to everyone.*

Amiable: *He is amiable and gracious.*

Funny: *Joe is funny.*

Generous: *My father is generous with his money.*

Gentle: *She is gentle with children.*

Brave: *Peter is brave, and Tom is humorous.*

Bright: *My nephew is bright.*

Broad-minded: *He is broad-minded and straightforward.*

Hard-working: *She is a very intelligent and hardworking student.*

Charming: *She is charming and beautiful.*

Humorous: *I think Tom is humorous.*

Sociable: *He is a sociable, reliable man.*

Others: communicative, compassionate, impartial, passionate, patient, persistent, polite, powerful, practical, pro-active, reliable, romantic, self-confident, self-disciplined, sincere, sociable, straightforward, sympathetic, thoughtful, tidy, tough, understanding, versatile, warmhearted, willing, witty , adaptable, fair-minded, passionate, adventurous, faithful, persistent, independent, romantic, considerate, intellectual, smart = intelligent, supportive, charitable, approachable.

PEOPLE DESCRIPTION MODEL ANSWER

SAMPLE 1:

Describe a person (you know), much older than you, who you admire.

You should say:

Who this person is

How you know this person

How this person has influenced you

And explain why you admire this person.

MODEL ANSWER:

Today I'm gonna talk about one of my favorite teachers who taught me at high school. Her name is Taylor. She had a great influence on me and was the most well-mannered person whom I look up to very much. Ms. Taylor taught me English for 3 years of high school. She was in her 40s, and she had a lot of teaching experience. In fact, we met each other almost every day since she was also my form teacher. She was always kind to students, treated us with respect and cared about us as if we had been her children. To be specific, she always brought some kinds of medicines so that whenever any student had a cold, cough or something like that, she would give them the medicines immediately.

Above all, the way she taught us in class influenced me the most. Her thoroughness and dedication in teaching inspired me to study English, even though I had not been interested in this foreign language before. Thanks to her inspiring teaching method, I was able to pass the university entrance exam with a high English grade. Moreover, she was very friendly and approachable, far more than I expected, in fact. She was willing to share her ideas and answer to all my questions. I was also influenced by her lifestyle, which was so worthy of respect and simple that I really wanted to imitate her. As she is a kind person, she always gave us the best advice and solutions about any problems we faced. From time to time, I felt that she was like my close friend who I could comfortably share everything with.

Although we have now all graduated from high school and have different goals to chase in life, we usually visit her at the weekends to share with her about our daily life at college.

SAMPLE 2:

Describe your good friend.

You should say:

Who this person is

Who long you have known them (= him or her)

Or, how you first met what you do together

And explain why you think this person is a good friend

MODEL ANSWER:

Speaking of a good friend, I would like to talk about Lucy, whom I have known for roughly 5 years. I first met her at university when she was my classmate. She was smart, confident, thoughtful, and always a straight A student who used to be nominated as the president of the student union because of her excellent academic performance. Moreover, she can always give me a helping hand and the most sincere advice whenever I am in need. For example, I remember when I didn't pass the mock university entrance exam, she consoled me, found the best ways to inspire me and made me more motivated in study and then we studied together until the official exam took place. Finally, with our effort we passed the entrance examination and studied at our favorite college.

At present, despite the fact that we have different plans and goals to pursue, I strongly believe that we will try our best to maintain this relationship and we will be best friends for good. Indeed, Lucy is a real friend of mine.

MODEL SENTENCES FOR PEOPLE DESCRIPTION

…I admire him/her from the bottom of my heart not only because of the person himself/herself, but also because of the things I learned from his/her words…

…I love/ impress/ admire my grandpa not only because of the person himself, but also because of the interesting, friendly, kind personality he has…

… His/her words influenced me a lot/very much…

…He/she never gives up easily…

…I hope that I will be able to become an inspirational person like him one day…

… He/she is a well-known investor/businessman…

… He/she has also made a great contribution to charity…

… He/she looks much younger than he/she actually is…

… He/she is of medium build and medium height….

…My father/grandpa/uncle is a very modern and interesting person….

…He/she is really into taking pictures, collecting antiques, and travelling around the world…

…He/she left me a lot of beautiful childhood memories…

…He/she took really good care of me when I was little; cooked me my favourite food, played with me, walked me to school and home, told me fairy tales, …

….My grandma/grandpa is a really nice person….

…. We have a lot in common and are like peas and carrots (get along very well together).....

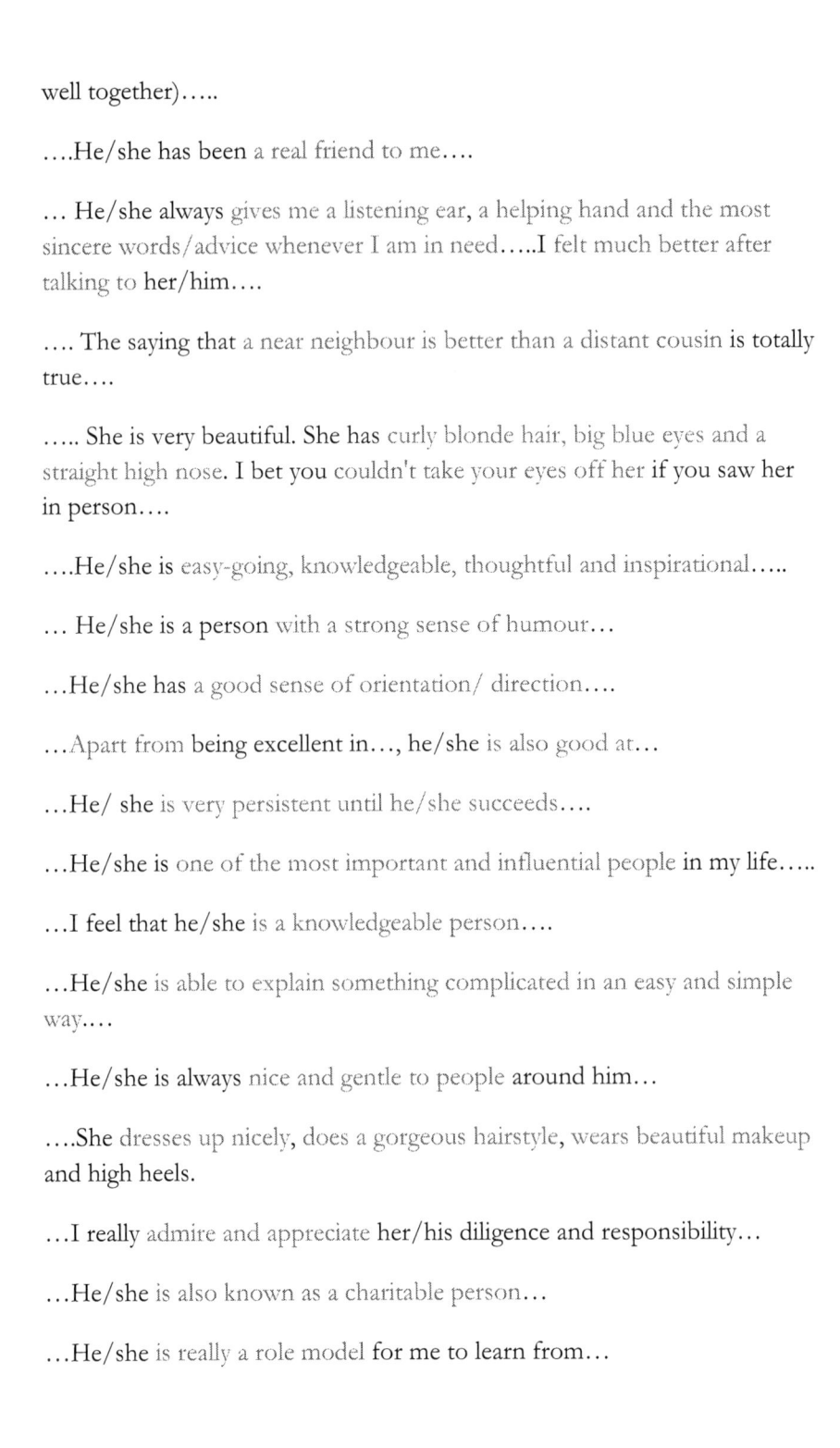

....He/she has been a real friend to me....

... He/she always gives me a listening ear, a helping hand and the most sincere words/advice whenever I am in need.....I felt much better after talking to her/him....

.... The saying that a near neighbour is better than a distant cousin is totally true....

..... She is very beautiful. She has curly blonde hair, big blue eyes and a straight high nose. I bet you couldn't take your eyes off her if you saw her in person....

....He/she is easy-going, knowledgeable, thoughtful and inspirational.....

... He/she is a person with a strong sense of humour...

...He/she has a good sense of orientation/ direction....

...Apart from being excellent in..., he/she is also good at...

...He/ she is very persistent until he/she succeeds....

...He/she is one of the most important and influential people in my life.....

...I feel that he/she is a knowledgeable person....

...He/she is able to explain something complicated in an easy and simple way....

...He/she is always nice and gentle to people around him...

....She dresses up nicely, does a gorgeous hairstyle, wears beautiful makeup and high heels.

...I really admire and appreciate her/his diligence and responsibility...

...He/she is also known as a charitable person...

...He/she is really a role model for me to learn from...

…He/she is able to get along well with all types of people…

…My mother has an eye for fashion. She usually keeps up with the latest fashion…

…He/she became successful after many years of writing songs/books…

…He/she tried to keep me entertained and find interesting things for us to do together…

…He/she has always taught me to be more patient and understanding towards other people…

PLACE DESCRIPTION

ANSWER ORDER:

1. What it is *(a shopping mall that/which is)*
2. Where it is *(near, close to, next to, across from, behind, on the corner of, at the end of the street, on X Street).*
3. When you first go there *(I first went there 10 years ago)*
4. What it looks like *(a crowded place -- being descriptive)*
5. What is it famous for *(this place is famous for/ this place is renowned for seafood, noodle, clean streets)*
6. Why do you visit this place *(because it provided me with something (delicious food, information, advice, etc./ I love going to the zoo because this gives me a chance to relax and see animals ("this" refers to "going to the zoo")/ ...because it reminds me of.../ because it lets me escape from daily life routines..../ .... because it makes me feel...)*
7. How do you feel about this place. *(My uncle's house is very important to me because I spend a lot of time there on the weekend/ I found this place very beautiful because it's so relaxing/ The sounds that you hear coming from the ocean are very soothing/ In fact, when I was there I watched two birds singing to each other....).*

ADJECTIVES FOR DESCRIBING PLACES

- **Enchanting:** *El Nido has been the most enchanting place I have ever visited.*

- **Attractive and enjoyable:** *We want to make the town a more attractive and enjoyable place for visitors.*

- **Stimulating:** *The swimming is stimulating.*

- **Cozy = inviting # uncomfortable:** *This coffee shop is cozy.*

- **Quiet = peaceful # bustling:** *Sometimes I need a quiet place to escape from my daily life routines.*

- **Vibrant = lively # boring:** *Art gallery is a lively place.*

- **Hectic:** *The restaurant is hectic.*

- **Boring = dull # fascinating**

- **Traditional = old-fashioned # modern**

- **Exhilarating**

- **Charming**

- **Impressive**

QUESTION ANALYSE:

Describe a place that your parent took you to

What sort of place it was *(a recreational area, a shopping mall, a restaurant, a cinema, a park, a religious building, a temple, etc.)*

How you got there *(my family and I took a bus…)*

Why your parents took you there (what is the reason: *vacation, to visit my uncle; attend my cousin's wedding…*)

Why you would or would not take your own children to this place *(if I had children, I'd take them here because I had a lot of fun/ because it's very beautiful/*

because I think they would have as much fun as I did.)

PLACE DESCRIPTION MODEL ANSWER

SAMPLE 1:

Describe a place with a lot of water (such as a river, a lake or the ocean) that you enjoyed visiting.

You should say:

Where this place was

What you did there

Why you went there

Who you went there with

And explain why you liked this place.

ANSWER:

I would like to talk about a place where my family went on a vacation last summer. It's called Binh Ba Island, which is located in Nha Trang city and I was really impressed with the beach there. The scenery along the coast was just breathtaking.

When we arrived at this destination, we had to take a ferry from the mainland, a journey which lasted roughly one hour. Fortunately, I was not seasick. When we reached there, surprisingly, the scenery appealed to me a lot, particularly the beach. The beach itself was absolutely breathtaking and the crystal clear water seemed to stretch endlessly to the horizon. Moreover, from a distance, huge waves were crashing onto the shore, which sounded like a melody. I was so excited that I just wanted to jump into the sea immediately.

On the beach, many people were enjoying the scenery, and some were swimming while their children were making sandcastles. My family quickly checked into the hotel, we changed our clothes and joined the people there.

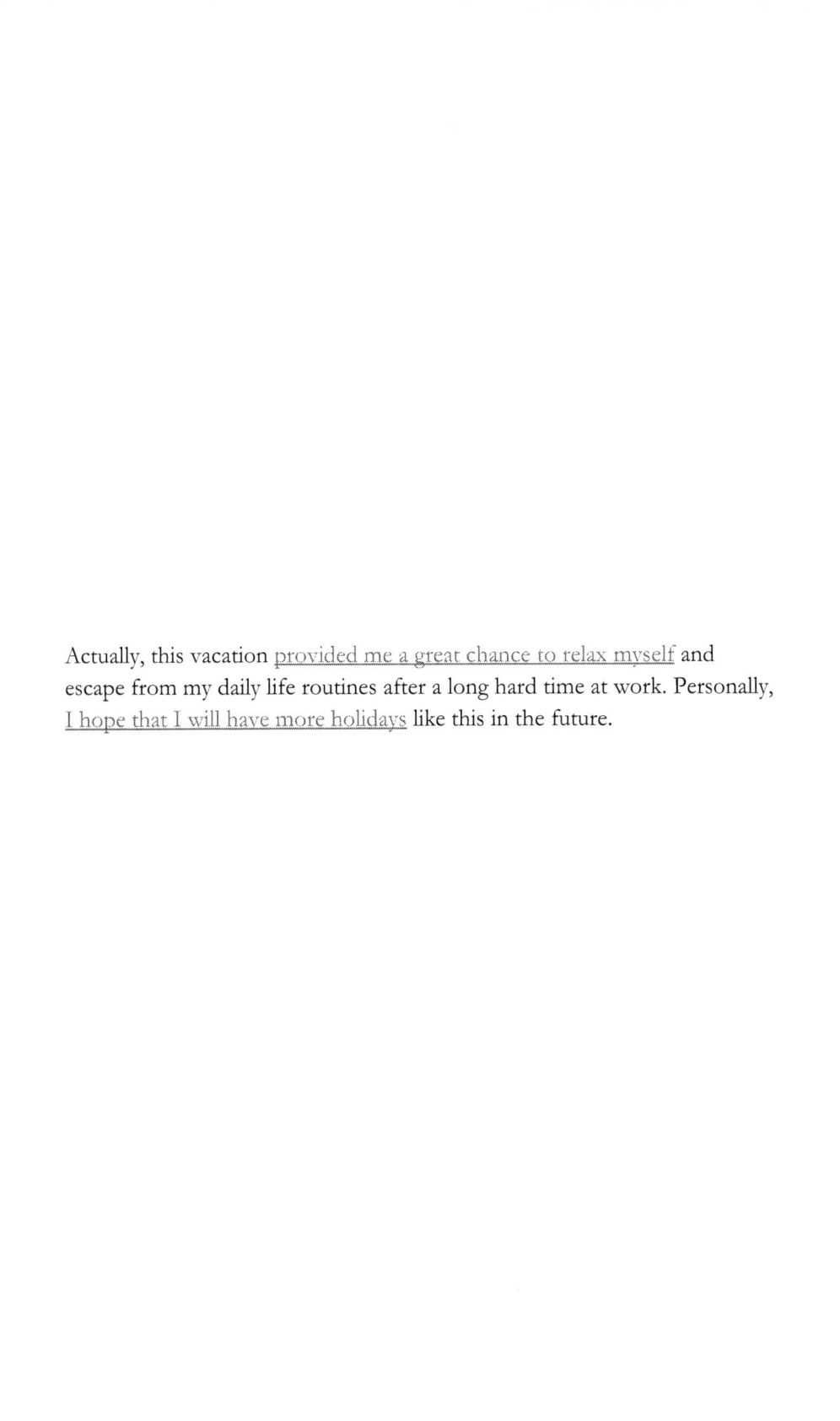

Actually, this vacation provided me a great chance to relax myself and escape from my daily life routines after a long hard time at work. Personally, I hope that I will have more holidays like this in the future.

SAMPLE 2:

Describe a quiet place.

Where it is

How often you visit there

What you do there

And explain the reason why you like or dislike the place.

ANSWER:

To me, quiet places mean libraries. But I'm not going to describe the library at my university as I still haven't visited it yet. The one I'm going to describe is the library at my high school in Sydney.

My school is very large and it consists of four big blocks named A, B, C, and D. The library occupies a small space on the highest floor in block D, and it's perhaps just about three or nearly four times as large as a normal classroom. There's a room used to store books and another for students to read books and self-study.

I spent most of my time in the library when I was in grade 10. The next two years were filled completely with competitions and extracurricular activities so I couldn't go to the library as often as before. I had my own favorite spot in the self-study section; it was the cubicle on the outermost row that is near the window, and whenever I visited the library to study or to read some borrowed books, I would choose that spot without any hesitation. I even wrote some words or symbols that I liked on the table; don't know whether they're still there now though.

I specifically chose this library to describe because it's really quiet, compared with some other libraries in Sydney that I've been to. It was really suitable for studying, and some students even went there to sleep! I had a great time self-studying in this library back then, I seriously would visit it again if I ever had a chance.

MODEL SENTENCES FOR PLACE DESCRIPTION

....Decoration style is classy and upscale....

....Atmosphere is cozy and comfy....

....Food is tasty and flavourful....

....The service is hospitable and speedy. All orders can be served in 10 minutes....

....The hotel was designed and constructed by the architects from South Africa, and took approximately ten years to complete....

....Food prices are affordable....

....Its location is convenient. It is easy to find a parking space....

....A customer can feel very comfy in such an environment....

....The restaurant is spacious. We can have different options when choosing a seat, and it also leaves some privacy for talking; it is pretty customer-oriented....

....The most impressive part about this spectacular building is its distinctive shape, which gives everyone an impression that a boat is sailing on the sea....

....What impressed me most was the hotel we stayed at....

....The hotel is definitely a unique symbol for Dubai....

....When I actually saw the hotel, I was totally amazed by it....

....The hotel gave us an impression that a boat was sailing on the sea....

....It makes the hotel iconic and unique....

….The library is situated in the center of the campus….

….The coffee house is located on a quiet street with a lot of trees planted on both sides….

….It is on the opposite side of my university….

….You can see a huge collection of books of different kinds: journals, academic books, magazines, newspapers….

….There is a cozy cafe on the top floor. It is great to sit down, enjoy the lovely campus view, and taste my favourite cappuccino while reading the book….

….When I was little, the room I loved the most was my bedroom….

….All the walls were painted light yellow, which made the room look elegant and subtle….

….My parents even hung a lot of photos of my family on the walls….

….This park is also a popular place for walking, jogging, flying a kite, playing hide-and-seek, having a picnic, dog walking, fishing…

….The scene is so spectacular when all the cherry blossoms are in full blossom in spring….

….The water is wonderfully clear….

….The most amazing scene is the time when cherry blossom petals fall down all over the river like snowflakes….

….It is the greatest place for relaxation….

….I love this park not only because of the park itself, but also because of the atmosphere I can soak up in the park….

….The room was equipped with central air-conditioning, satellite TV and internet access, which was very convenient….

….This place is quite private….

…. This is a lively, fashionable and cosmopolitan place…..

….A lot of public events and private parties are held in this place as well….

….The restaurant I would like to talk about is called Pizza Hut, which is a western-style restaurant, specializing in pizza and spaghetti. It is one of the most popular and famous restaurants in Japanese nowadays….

….Well, the foreign country that I would like to visit is the UK, which is one of the most attractive and fascinating travelling destinations for many backpackers, and I am no exception….

….It is also an ideal place for me to meet and chat with my relatives….

OBJECT DESCRIPTION

Something that comes up in part 2 speaking is talking about objects, talking about <u>things that you own</u> like *a watch, a smartphone, a motorbike, etc.* When we talk about an object, we need to describe its appearance.

How do we describe its appearance? We describe it by <u>using adjectives</u>. But you know, there are a lot of things you can say about objects. We can talk about what we think about it. *Is it beautiful? Is it lovely? Is it ugly?*…We can talk about *its size*, we can be general, we can say <u>*big*</u>, <u>*small*</u>, <u>*tiny*</u>…we can be specific (3 centimeter long, 2 feet long…). We can talk about *its age* like <u>new</u>, <u>old</u>, <u>brand-new</u>, <u>twelve years old</u>; we can talk about *its shape, color*; we can also talk about *its pattern*; we can talk about *its origin (where is it from?)*; we can talk about *its material (wood, bamboo, metal..)*

<u>Made of & made from</u>: these prepositions are very important.

We use **made of** when we can <u>still recognize the material</u> that is used to make the object.

<u>For example</u>: *the house is <u>made of</u> wood.*

We use **made from** when we <u>don't know what material is used</u> to make the object.

<u>For example</u>: *Plastic is <u>made from</u> oil.*

When we are talking about the description about where we got something, or how we found something, we are going to talk about the past, but we don't just stick with past simple, and past simple. We should be saying something like *"I was visiting my family when my brother surprised me with a new watch"* or sorts of reasons (ways to talk about **why** or **what** was your object is used by using *infinitive of purpose "to; in order to; so as to"*), and then we can talk about <u>when was the first time</u>, <u>when was the last time</u> we saw or used something. For example *"the first time I used this computer when I was 10 years old"*, *"the last time I saw the watch is when I was at my parents' home"*; *"the last time I played the video game was with my brother at Christmas 4 years ago"*, and then we will talk about <u>how this object made us or other people feel?</u> You might talk about the birthday present you received or you might talk about the birthday present you gave. Either way, there will be interested how you feel about giving it or how the other feels about getting it. In this case, you should talk about <u>what the object looks like</u>, but you also talk about what other people feel, and why other people do things by <u>using adjectives of evaluation</u> *"people watch TV because it's relaxing"*, *"people like to read because it's enjoyable"* we use adjectives of evaluation to talk about <u>what we feel</u>, and <u>how we feel</u>.

USEFUL ADJECTIVES FOR DESCRIBING OBJECTS

Opinion: good, wonderful, splendid, pretty, fantastic, awful, ugly, dirty, comfortable, uncomfortable, wasteful, valuable, worthless, worthy, useful, useless, important, scarce, rare, lovely, disgusting, amazing, loathsome, surprising, usual, unusual, etc.

Touch: hard, silky, soft, smooth, polished, grainy, rough, glossy, glassy, etc.

Size, weight: heavy, small, tiny, little, light, big, tall, fat, short, slender, thin, underweight, wide, enormous, vast, giant, huge, great, slim, etc.

Smell: perfumed, smelly, noxious, aromatic, fragrant, scented, etc.

Temperature: hot, cold, icy, freezing, frigid, etc.

Age: old, young, baby, teenage, adolescent, antique, ancient, youthful, old-fashioned, elderly, mature, modern, recent, etc.

Shape: round, circular, triangular, square, oval, spherical, sleek, straight, wavy, etc.

Brightness: light, bright, dark, shining, dull, pale, glowing, gleaming, luminous, etc.

Color: blue, black, purple, white, red, pink, orange, dark green, yellowish, gray, silver, brown, transparent, colorless, etc.

Material: cloth, fabric, concrete, ceramic, metal, china, cotton, glass, plastic, wooden, steel, leather, silicon,...

OBJECT DESCRIPTION MODEL ANSWER

Describe a product you bought that you were (or, are) happy with.

You should say:

What you bought

How you bought it

Why you bought it

And explain why you were (or are) happy with it.

MODEL ANSWER 1:

I would like to talk about a household appliance which <u>plays an integral part</u> of my daily life, and <u>makes me very satisfied with</u>; that is a washing machine.

<u>Thanks to the simple instructions</u>, and this machine is <u>very easy to use</u>, my family members and I use it every day to wash our laundries such as clothing or sheets.

Personally, I think this machine <u>is quite beneficial to me due to its convenience</u>. <u>To be specific</u>, instead of spending nearly an hour on cleaning clothing by hand, it takes me only 5 minutes to put all the clothing in a washing machine. <u>Moreover</u>, my clothes washer has a large capacity up to 15kg so I can run a load of clothing through it at one time <u>in order to</u> save both water and time. <u>As a result</u>, I can save a huge amount of time <u>in order to</u> do other household chores or even learn new things that <u>I'm interested in</u>; <u>for example</u>, I can learn foreign languages or cooking.

<u>In addition</u>, a washing machine can dry clothing automatically; <u>therefore</u>, I don't have to worry about my clothing will be wet in the rainy season or winter.

<u>As a final point, I would say that</u> the washing machine is one of the greatest inventions of the industrial revolution that brings various benefits for me

39

and other people using it.

MODEL ANSWER 2:

I would like to talk about a Samsung smart phone which I bought last summer and I was really satisfied with it. This cell phone was the latest product from Samsung, so there were various useful applications such as video calling, camera, Zalo chat, emails, games, music players, and so on. I would use this smart phone to listen to music, make phone calls, send messages and check emails. I must say that this portable device helps me a lot no matter where I am.

There were various reasons why I loved this product. Firstly, I would use it for entertainment purposes. What I mean is I could refresh myself after a long hard day at work by listening to my favorite music or enjoying action movies online. Moreover, thanks to this smart phone, I was able to keep in touch with my old friends whom I didn't often have a chance to meet in person. In addition, this mobile phone helped me to handle my workload effectively. For example, I could check and send emails or write my essays when waiting for the bus, which saved a huge amount of my time.

At present, I still use this smart phone every day for my work, study, and entertainment purposes. I think that this is an indispensable product in my daily life routines.

MODEL SENTENCES FOR OBJECT DESCRIPTION

....I love it because it can release my stress, relieve my pressure and put me in a good mood....

....It was super thin and incredibly light....

....I was totally impressed by....

....It is a photo of my whole family sitting around the table having New Year's Dinner....

....The photo always reminds me of the meal my mom cooked and the words my father said before the dinner....

....I love it not only because of the toy itself, but also the sentimental value it has to me....

....Its color is super eye-catching....

....It was an original oil painting on canvas....

....I remember that the first time I read the book was around October 2010....

....I am interested in this vehicle for a number of reasons....

....This vehicle is quite fashionable and trendy....

....The quality is reliable and trustworthy....

....Its price is affordable....

....The one I choose is my baby girl doll, which was one of my favorite toys as a child....

....I didn't actually buy this smartphone because it would be too expensive for me to afford. It was a gift from my uncle....

....The church is made of red brick, and the architecture, as I said before, is in the old French style....

....A folding chair is convenient for me because my room is small and I don't have space for a lot of furniture....

....When I first saw the bicycle I was very excited....

....It was a birthday present from my parents....

....It has various applications like video chat, digital camera, wireless Internet, and games. It's easy to share photos and music....

....I use this smartphone for almost everything, it even has a calendar that reminds me about appointments....

....This smartphone is an essential part of my life. I couldn't live without it....

....This Lego car was a birthday present from my parents....

....Last summer I bought a new smartphone and I am very satisfied with it....

....The most important thing is that this smartphone is very easy to use....

....There were numerous reasons why I took an interest in this smartphone. Firstly, I would like to use it for entertainment purposes....

....This household appliance plays an important role in my daily life....

....The coat is made of cotton only and by a Japanese clothes brand....

PAST EVENT DESCRIPTION

ANSWER ORDER:

1. What it was *(a historic event, a party, a ceremony, a wedding, a bicycle tour, a family holiday, a vacation, a kind of weather, a TV program, a football match, summer camp, school trip etc.)*
2. When it happened *(last week, last month, last year, in December, since I was a teenager, 2 years ago, on my parents' 20th wedding anniversary, at Christmas, etc.)*
3. Where it happened *(in the countryside, on the street, at the university, at my uncle's house, at a restaurant, etc.)*
4. What happened *(dancing, singing, drinking, playing games, telling jokes, cooking, etc.)*
5. Who was there *(my family, friends, teachers, neighbors, classmates, farmers, my cousin, etc.)*
6. How you feel/felt about it *(relaxing, enjoyable, valuable, special, embarrassed, moved, delighted, thrilled, enthusiastic, satisfied etc.)*

PAST EVENT DESCRIPTION MODEL ANSWER

SAMPLE 1:

Describe a sporting event that you have attended.

You should say:

What kind of sporting event it was

When the event took place

What you did there & who was with you

And explain how you felt about it.

MODEL ANSWER:

I'm gonna talk about an absurd boxing match that I along with my best friend went to watch last week. To be honest, since I realized that I was quite physically unfit, and I thought that I should take up regular exercise, so I have taken up boxing to get into shape. This has led me to develop my fondness for this kind of sport, and I decided to go and watch a real bout.

As it was the final of the local competition, the two contestants were both extremely competent. While we were waiting for the boxers to come into the ring, crowds of spectators started to cheer and chant enthusiastically to show their support for the two fighters, which created an exciting atmosphere of participation. 15 minutes later, the boxers appeared. They looked incredibly muscular, and this made me green with envy of their athletic physique.

Since boxing involves a high possibility of injury, on safety grounds both athletes were sufficiently equipped with essential sports gear for their protection, which may be one reason why the sport continues to thrive, despite the dangers. After the introduction and rules reminder, the contest started. It was interesting that the two participants were equally talented, so they had to really exert themselves to win. However, just at the height of the contest, one boxer got a cramp and tripped unexpectedly. The fall was so sudden that he couldn't react and ended up spraining his wrist. Although it was not a life-threatening injury, it did prevent him from continuing the fight. The other fighter was then declared the winner. Everybody was at a loss for words, and I have to say that was the most interesting match I've ever seen! It was a little disappointing, but also funny and fascinating in a way.

Personally, this match was quite entertaining and valuable for me. I learnt a lot of remarkable skills from the boxers; they were so professional. I hope I will be as skillful as they are, and I will definitely practice my skills regularly from now.

SAMPLE 2:

Describe a time you had good experience in the countryside

You should say

Where it was

When it was

What you did

And explain why you liked/disliked the experience

MODEL ANSWER:

Although I live in a very hectic city, I also feel connected to the countryside. Life in the rural areas always brings me a sense of tranquility. Last summer, I got away from the overcrowded city by spending all the time with my grandparents in the country. This experience has been a great memory for me to look back on with fondness.

Well, as you can imagine, country life is quite different from that of the city, and living in the countryside is sometimes really challenging. While in my city apartment, all I have to do is just some light housework like washing dishes or cleaning the bathroom, but in the countryside, I have to take care of the garden every day and even help out with farm work. My grandparents have instructed me to do this because it will help to develop self-reliance. Although there are some hardships involved, finishing these tasks brings me closer to nature and I have gradually become more adaptable to changes. Besides, without the distraction of the Internet, I found myself more open to people around me and understand them better. I have come to realize that alienation between humans nowadays is partly caused by the dominance of technology.

Despite getting back to my normal life in the city, I still find the time spent in the countryside very memorable. I believe that thanks to the precious time spent in my grandparents' country home, I have become more mature and dependable.

SAMPLE 3:

Describe a time you talked to a stranger

You should say:

Who the person was

Where the conversation took place

What the conversation was about

And explain why you found the conversation exciting.

MODEL ANSWER:

Last month, on the flight to Tokyo, I had a chance to talk to a British environmentalist, and I have to say that it was a very memorable conversation. During the conversation, she enlightened me as to the seriousness of our environmental problems. Practically, she said that the relentless exploitation of human beings has depleted a lot of natural resources, such as forests, water, plants and, of course, fossil fuels. Moreover, problems like global warming also stem from various kinds of pollution, the most severe of which is air pollution. Undoubtedly, these environmental problems would be extremely detrimental to our health, and affect overall standards of living and quality of life.

When I asked her about how to alleviate such environmental problems, she said the decisive factor is our awareness. People should bear in mind that every action they take will directly affect the overall environment, in either positive or negative ways. She advised me to reduce my personal carbon footprint by cutting down on car emissions if I have access to public transport. She also gave me tips on saving energy as an essential way to put a stop to environmental degradation. Although we had just met, she was really helpful and friendly towards me, and I think that my talk with her was really informative.

MODEL SENTENCES FOR PAST EVENT DESCRIPTION

…..The occasion when I was angry was several months ago when I was about to board a flight at the airport…..

…..Our flight would be delayed due to the snowstorm/lightning/dense fog…..

…..The telephone conversation I would like to talk about is…..

…..At first, I felt extremely nervous since it was my first interview. I lacked confidence…..

…..During the conversation, however, I found the interviewer called Michael was fairly gentle and nice…..

…..Afterwards, I felt that she was satisfied with my performance…..

…..I started to skip class because I found it was boring…..

…..My mom was so happy that she decided to give me a surprise…..

…..I felt a sense of fulfillment. I was really impressed with my mother's special gift and it gave me a lasting memory…..

…..The wedding ceremony I would like to share with you is…..

…..Mike and I have been close friends since childhood. Therefore, when he invited me to be his best man, I agreed without any hesitation…..

…..We had a memorable and busy day back then…..

…..Before the ceremony, we had laboriously decorated and planned everything…..

…..It was one of the most unforgettable moments of my life…..

…..I was greatly frustrated and hopeless. I have never experienced something as difficult as that in my life…..

…..The exciting experience I would like to tell you about happened several years ago when I was a college student…..

…..There were two options for me which was whether to continue my study or to get a job right away. It was a really difficult choice that I had to make…..

…..I would like to talk about an occasion when I got up extremely early…..

…..I would like to tell you about the first paid job that I really enjoyed in my life…..

…..I really enjoy doing this work for some reasons….. the job gives me countless opportunities to improve my English skills…..

…..I learnt to swim when I was a small child because my parents believed that it would be useful for me…..

…..Swimming improves the health and helps me to avoid illness…..

…..I would like to tell you about a special meal on my 18th birthday party, which was cooked at home by my mother…..

…..For me, this was the most special meal in my life…..

…..I would like to tell you about the trip that I went on last summer, to the hometown of my classmate…..

…..I'm going to talk about my brother's wedding day, which took place several years ago in the town where I grew up…..

…..I would like to tell you about a situation that made me angry was getting stuck in a traffic jam…..

CONCLUSION

Thank you again for downloading this book on *"IELTS Speaking Part 2 Strategies: The Ultimate Guide with Tips, Tricks and Practice on How to Get a Target Band Score of 8.0+ in 10 Minutes a Day."* and reading all the way to the end. I'm extremely grateful.

If you know of anyone else who may benefit from the useful strategies, structures, tips, Speaking Part 2 language in this book, please help me inform them of this book. I would greatly appreciate it.

Finally, if you enjoyed this book and feel that it has added value to your work and study in any way, please take a couple of minutes to share your thoughts and post a REVIEW on Amazon. Your feedback will help me to continue to write other books of IELTS topic that helps you get the best results. Furthermore, if you write a simple REVIEW with positive words for this book on Amazon, you can help hundreds or perhaps thousands of other readers who may want to improve their English speaking sounding like a native speaker. Like you, they worked hard for every penny they spend on books. With the information and recommendation you provide, they would be more likely to take action right away. We really look forward to reading your review.

Thanks again for your support and good luck!

If you enjoy my book, please write a POSITIVE REVIEW on Amazon.

-- Rachel Mitchell --

CHECK OUT OTHER BOOKS

Go here to check out other related books that might interest you:

Shortcut To English Collocations: Master 2000+ English Collocations In Used Explained Under 20 Minutes A Day

https://www.amazon.com/dp/B06W2P6S22

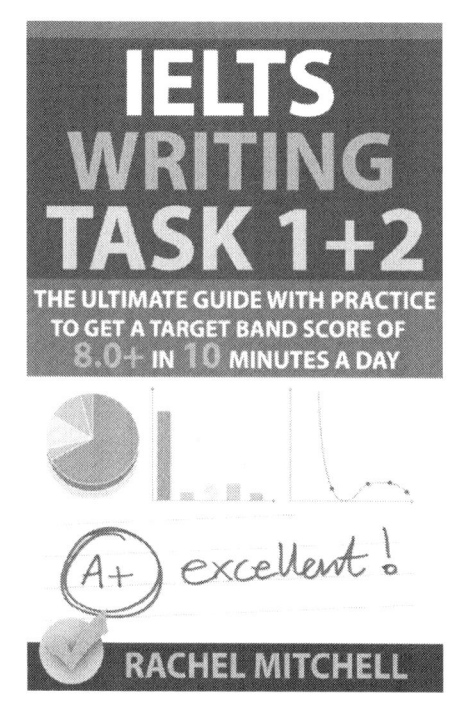

IELTS Writing Task 1 + 2: The Ultimate Guide with Practice to Get a Target Band Score of 8.0+ In 10 Minutes a Day

https://www.amazon.com/dp/B075DFYPG6

Common English Mistakes Explained With Examples: Over 600 Mistakes Almost Students Make and How to Avoid Them in Less Than 5 Minutes A Day

https://www.amazon.com/dp/B072PXVHNZ

Paraphrasing Strategies: 10 Simple Techniques For Effective Paraphrasing In 5 Minutes Or Less

https://www.amazon.com/dp/B071DFG27Q

Legal Vocabulary In Use: Master 600+ Essential Legal Terms And
Phrases Explained In 10 Minutes A Day

http://www.amazon.com/dp/B01L0FKXPU

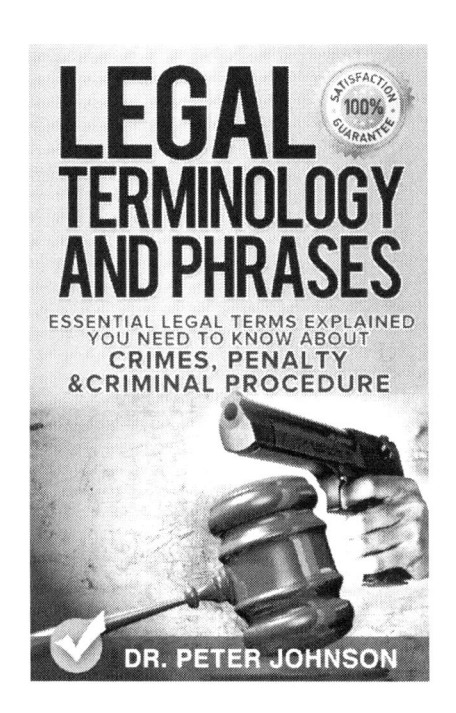

Legal Terminology And Phrases: Essential Legal Terms Explained You Need To Know About Crimes, Penalty And Criminal Procedure

http://www.amazon.com/dp/B01L5EB54Y

Productivity Secrets For Students: The Ultimate Guide To Improve Your Mental Concentration, Kill Procrastination, Boost Memory And Maximize Productivity In Study

http://www.amazon.com/dp/B01JS52UT6

Daughter of Strife: 7 Techniques On How To Win Back Your Stubborn Teenage Daughter

https://www.amazon.com/dp/B01HS5E3V6

Parenting Teens With Love And Logic: A Survival Guide To Overcoming The Barriers Of Adolescence About Dating, Sex And Substance Abuse

https://www.amazon.com/dp/B01JQUTNPM

Understanding Men in Relationships: The Top 44 Irresistible Qualities Men Want In A Woman.

https://www.amazon.com/dp/B01MQWI11G

Printed in Great Britain
by Amazon